The Advanced Technology Program

The Advanced Technology Program

A Case Study in Federal Technology Policy

Loren Yager and Rachel Schmidt

The AEI Press

Publisher for the American Enterprise Institute
WASHINGTON, D.C.

1997

The views expressed in this volume are those of the authors and do not necessarily represent the views of the General Accounting Office or the Congressional Budget Office. The authors would like to thank Arthur Alexander, Claude Barfield, Jim Bothwell, Ed Dale, Emil Friberg, Bob Hunt, Douglas Irwin, Dick Neu, Elliot Schwartz, Bill Thomas, Andy Vogelsang, and Scott Wallsten for their thoughtful comments on earlier drafts. Despite the assistance of reviewers, the authors are solely responsible for this analysis.

Distributed to the Trade by National Book Network, 15200 NBN Way, Blue Ridge Summit, PA 17214. To order call toll free 1-800-462-6420 or 1-717-794-3800. For all other inquiries please contact the AEI Press, 1150 Seventeenth Street, N.W., Washington, D.C. 20036 or call 1-800-862-5801.

ISBN 0-8447-7102-3 (paper)

1 3 5 7 9 10 8 6 4 2

THE AEI PRESS
Publisher for the American Enterprise Institute
1150 17th Street, N.W., Washington, D.C. 20036

Contents

CONTENTS

Foreword

The Commerce Department's Advanced Technology Program emerged in 1993 as the centerpiece of the Clinton administration's attempt to forge a new public technology policy for the United States. Over the past five years, the ATP has spent over $1 billion in matching grants to almost 300 individual firms and consortia. And originally, before meeting strong opposition from majority congressional Republicans after the 1994 elections, the Clinton administration projected annual appropriations by 1998 of at least $750 million. Attempts by congressional opponents to zero out the ATP failed in the 1996 budget standoff between President Clinton and the Republicans.

In fiscal 1997, the program received $250 million, and the president is requesting an appropriation of $275 million for fiscal 1998.

At whatever level it is funded, the ATP will remain at the center of controversy. President Clinton continues to espouse a strong commitment to the effort, and congressional opponents still firmly believe that it is an egregious example of "corporate welfare." A problem for both sides is that any economic benefits from the program will emerge slowly and will be widely diffused. With this difficulty in mind, this study, by Loren Yager and Rachel Schmidt, does not attempt to measure benefits and costs; rather, the authors review the program's economic rationale and the project-selection criteria set forth in its legislation, regulations, and administrative notices and ask whether the criteria in fact lead to projects promising substantial social benefits in excess of private returns on investment—that is, projects that appear worthwhile for the economy as a whole that are nevertheless unlikely to attract private investment.

Based on their analysis, the authors conclude that the ATP "has had only limited success" in selecting projects that could not obtain funding from the private sector. They point to two reasons for this failure. First, the "goals of government and firms conflict." The government's rationale should drive it toward projects in which the private sector has little interest, but the firms have little interest in proposing projects that differ significantly from the projects they pursue for profit. Second, they find that "there is no common ground between many of the political and the economic requirements of a successful program." One way to resolve the issue would target areas where appropriability is most difficult and restrict intellectual property protection. Here, however, the "economic importance to the government of disseminating results widely and without cost runs into the political opposition of the firms and risks providing benefits to foreign firms—a potentially embarrassing outcome politically."

In short, they conclude, "it appears that the overlap between programs that expand social benefits and those that are politically successful is very small indeed."

CLAUDE E. BARFIELD
Director, Science and Technology Policy Studies
American Enterprise Institute

1
Introduction

The past four years have been turbulent ones for federal research and development (R&D) policy in the United States. In 1993, the Clinton administration advocated an explicit technology policy as a means of promoting economic growth and a higher standard of living (White House 1993, 26–36). Most notably, this policy took the form of larger direct federal investments in applied R&D projects. But elections in 1994 brought a new Republican majority to Congress, and in 1996, the public reaffirmed that decision. Together with renewed attention to reducing the federal budget deficit, Congress's opposition to direct government spending on commercial R&D could mean the demise of administration efforts to fund applied R&D projects.

One such effort is the Advanced Technology Program (ATP), run by the National Institute of Standards and Technology (NIST) of the Department of Commerce. The ATP was first appropriated $10 million in 1990, and annual funding reached as high as $340 million for FY 1995. The Clinton administration proposed increasing ATP's annual funding to more than twice that amount by FY 1997, but Congress had other priorities: out of a FY 1996 request of $491 million, the House of Representatives initially voted to provide no funding for the program, and Congress ultimately appropriated less than half the proposed amount. By the time the president submitted his FY 1997 budget request, his proposal for the ATP had been scaled back to $345 million. But once again, Congress chose to appropriate less: $225 million. The president's budget request for FY 1998 included an increase of $50 million for that appropriation.

ATP's main goal is to stimulate applied R&D projects in the private sector by providing matching grants to companies or consortia that develop technologies useful across industries (so-called generic technologies). To counter the criticism that federal subsidies are subject to pork-barrel politics, program administrators have tried to shield the process of granting awards from political influence. ATP has also tried to avoid duplication of effort by encouraging participants to collaborate with other companies, universities, and federal laboratories. Firms that participate in ATP must have a vested interest—award recipients are required to pay at least half their project costs.

Despite a lively debate over its future, with theoretical arguments on both sides, critics and proponents alike have paid little attention to how the program has been carried out. That is unfortunate, because the ATP provides an interesting experiment to test whether the federal government can promote economic growth through an explicit technology policy.

Naturally, there are many conceptual challenges in assessing technology programs. What metrics should one use to evaluate the success of federal R&D? The profits that a firm earns as a result of an innovation are a useful place to start, but should the evaluation also include reduced profits from firms that face greater competition because of the new technology? And given that the ATP targets generic technologies, how do we measure the gains that other industries also realize as a result of the research?

There are other practical difficulties as well. Since the ATP began just six years ago with a relatively small amount of funding, only a few projects have been around long enough to evaluate. And those evaluations would necessarily be preliminary, since one might easily expect ten years to elapse between the point at which a project is

2

funded and its ultimate use in a commercial product or process. During that time, many other factors could influence the development of the technology or the success of the firm, making it hard to judge what role government funding played.

A second practical problem is that the Advanced Technology Program has changed in structure since the time at which the first projects were funded. That would mean that a project's outcome may not provide useful guidance for the program today. Beginning in 1994, administrators of the ATP changed their strategy for making awards to emphasize "focus areas"—groups of projects in a targeted field of technology that receive blocks of $10 million to $50 million annually for five or more years. Program managers changed their approach because they believed that federal funding would be more effective if the funding were more concentrated in specific fields of technology. But that shift from allowing the pool of applicants to determine the research agenda to targeting focus areas is exactly the type of change that would make findings on the results of early project selections less generalizable to today's awards.

With those hurdles in mind, people might be tempted to throw up their hands rather than begin an evaluation of the ATP. But there are other ways to examine how well this experiment in technology policy is working. The first section of this volume summarizes the economic rationales for government support of R&D and compares them with the reasons that Congress created the ATP. But even the best of rationales does not ensure a program's success. For that reason, the second part of the volume looks closely at how the government is trying to carry out the program and examines the question of whether, even with good faith and insulation from political pressures, a successful implementation is possible. While it is too early to judge results of specific projects, the documents and other materials of the ATP provide a fertile ground for such an examination. They are the means by which the original rationales were translated into regulations for ATP administrators, and they lead to a discovery of the dilemmas and contradictions seemingly inherent in the program. After examining those documents, we argue that it is unlikely that the ATP can meet the conditions necessary for success: selecting projects with large returns to the nation and funding only those projects that would not otherwise find private financing.

2
Is There a Rationale for ATP?

The federal government has long influenced private spending on R&D through its macroeconomic, tax, trade, patent, and antitrust policies. It has also provided direct funding to universities, national laboratories, and private firms to conduct R&D for a variety of reasons. These include conducting basic research, developing goods for federal procurement, setting technology standards, and disseminating know-how. More recent rationales for direct R&D spending, however, are geared explicitly toward bolstering economic growth within the civil sector.

Traditional Rationales for Federal Funding of R&D

Traditional justifications for a federal role in R&D relate to the fact that much of the benefit cannot be captured or "appropriated" by the firm that conducts the research. Often the benefits of one firm's research "spill over" to others that, without investing much in the know-how, nevertheless learn about its results. Since it is difficult to keep an exclusive hold on technology, the social benefits of R&D are often greater than the returns to any individual firm that undertakes it. As a result, the private sector will invest too little in R&D relative to what is socially optimal.

Sponsoring Basic Research. Federal spending has traditionally supported fields that have very broad social benefits such as basic research and some work in public health and nutrition, energy conservation, and environmental protection. Those fields are characterized by the inability of firms to capture fully the returns from an investment and by a high degree of inherent uncertainty. Since it is particularly hard to limit access to fundamental break-throughs in the knowledge base (that is, spillovers are sub-stantial), basic research is a more extreme example of a situation where the returns to R&D are not appropriable. Indeed, public policy and academic culture tend to sup-port disseminating basic research findings as widely as possible because of their broad social benefits.

While the general outlines of this argument are well accepted, little consensus exists among economists on where to draw the line with the appropriability argument. Some see basic research as the only clear case where gov-ernment spending is justified, while others point out that it is hard to know where basic research ends and applied work begins (Branscomb 1992, 25). In addition, private firms have funded a substantial share of basic research without any government intervention (BEA 1994, 62). This suggests that the appropriability argument is more useful as a general rationale for government support of basic research than as a guide for specific policy choices.

Developing Goods for Federal Procurement. The bulk of federal R&D funding is used to develop new products or processes that the government plans to procure. National defense provides the best example. In FY 1997, funding for research, development, test, and evaluation (RDT&E) within the Department of Defense (DOD) totaled more than $37 billion (table 2–1). Although its share has de-clined in recent years, DOD still accounts for around half of all federal R&D expenditures. More than 95 percent of DOD's R&D funding supports applied or advanced devel-opment projects rather than basic research, and most of that work is performed by the private sector. Although DOD has had a strong influence on many high-technol-ogy industries such as aerospace, traditionally its invest-

TABLE 2–1

R&D Investments by Agency, FY 1997–FY 1998

(current billions of budget authority)

Agency	FY 1997 Estimate	FY 1997 Share (%)	FY 1998 Request	FY 1998 Share (%)
Defense	37.5	51	36.8	49
Health and Human Services	12.9	18	13.5	18
NASA	9.3	13	9.6	13
Energy	6.2	8	7.3	10
National Science Foundation	2.5	3	2.6	3
Agriculture	1.5	2	1.5	2
Commerce	1.1	1	1.1	1
Interior	0.6	1	0.6	1
Transportation	0.6	1	0.8	1
EPA	0.5	1	0.6	1
Other	1.2	2	1.2	2
Totals	73.8	100	75.5	100

Source: Budget of the U.S. Government, FY 1998, p. 78.

ments have not been made explicitly to promote economic growth.

The Department of Defense is the largest source of federal R&D spending. DOD, the Department of Health and Human Services (which includes research grants from the National Institutes of Health), the National Aeronautics and Space Administration, and the Department of Energy account for about 90 percent of federal funding for R&D.

Those research efforts have indirectly assisted U.S. industries, as some innovations developed originally for government procurement have proved to have commercial markets as well. In that sense, government-sponsored R&D has been a boon—government R&D support and the surety of a federal procurement market encouraged private firms to develop innovations that they might other-

7

wise have avoided or pursued at a slower pace.[1] And now that declines in military spending have led to consolidations in some industries, defense officials and Congress have begun to consider the economic repercussions of DOD's R&D and procurement spending more explicitly.

Setting Standards and Disseminating Know-How. A few long-standing cases exist where the federal government has explicitly aimed to support commercial economic growth. One such example is the traditional role played by the National Institute of Standards and Technology (formerly, the National Bureau of Standards)—setting standards for measurement and interoperability within a technological field or industry. Standards encourage firms to develop compatible products and processes, which, in turn, improve the efficiency of their use.

As in the case of basic research, R&D on setting standards for an industry is a field where, unless a business dominates a market with its technology, any firm that makes the investment is unlikely to capture much of the benefit. Industry trade associations or consortia can be quite effective at establishing standards without federal assistance. Nonetheless, in some cases, government intervention in setting industry standards may be warranted.

Improving the Performance of Industries

Under those traditional rationales, federal support for R&D has been part of U.S. policy throughout the postwar period. Over the past two decades, however, the federal government has become more actively involved in policies that explicitly aim to promote economic growth.[2]

The impetus for a new technology policy can be traced to changes in the U.S. and global economies. During the 1970s, domestic indicators of economic performance—and especially of productivity growth—slowed considerably from rates that prevailed in previous decades. During the 1980s, economic indicators such as the large U.S. trade deficit and the poor trade performance of individual sectors created additional concerns. Although the strong dollar was a more important factor behind the relative decline of U.S. manufacturing industries, tremendous growth in the Japanese automobile and semiconductor industries helped create the perception that government policy—particularly, the Japanese government's sectoral policies—had much to do with their success. A related concern was that while the preeminence of the United States in basic research was intact, U.S. businesses were less effective than foreign competitors at turning scientific discoveries into marketable products and processes (Council on Competitiveness 1991, 2–3).

Those forces culminated in political pressure to promote domestic industries, especially high-technology ones, through a variety of trade and technology policies such as changes in tax laws to favor R&D investment (for example, the Research and Experimentation Tax Credit in 1981), clarification of antitrust laws to facilitate research joint ventures (the National Cooperative Research Act in 1984, for example), and direct government financing to establish a consortium of semiconductor manufacturers (such as Sematech in 1988). Many of those policies, particularly import restraints of various kinds, focused on industries that had previously been major strengths of the U.S. economy, including automobiles, steel, machine tools, and semiconductors.

The Omnibus Trade and Competitiveness Act of 1988 is probably the most important example of how international competitive pressures led to explicit policies aimed at improving the performance of U.S. industries. That massive piece of legislation includes numerous titles related to trade and technology policies, including two and a half pages that established the Advanced Technology Program (U.S. Congress 1988).

A review of that legislation suggests that in addition

to the traditional rationales, three other justifications were used to argue for direct federal spending on commercial R&D projects: the long-term and high-risk nature of applied R&D, a perceived lack of collaboration among U.S. firms, and the notion that governments can improve the nation's standard of living by strategically supporting certain industries (strategic trade theory).

Promoting Long-Term and High-Risk R&D. Congress stated its goals most clearly when it wrote that the ATP was established "for the purpose of assisting United States businesses in creating and applying generic technology and research results" (U.S. Congress 1988, sec. 28 [a]). But which technologies are generic, and what led Congress to believe that U.S. businesses needed help in applying the results of research?

In recent years, analysts have argued that a sort of myopia has set in among U.S. businesses: they have focused consistently on quick returns and have thus made poor investment choices. For example, the Clinton administration contends that shorter product life cycles and pressure to realize near-term gains have kept firms from sufficient investment in risky or longer-term research, especially R&D that may not bear fruit for five to seven years (National Science and Technology Council 1995, 62). This claim is similar to the more general argument that U.S. capital markets are too impatient; venture capitalists, some contend, are willing to invest only in projects that are at or near the prototype stage and to which other investors are similarly reluctant to make the necessary long-term commitments.

A somewhat different issue is that raising funds from outside investors for R&D efforts may be particularly problematic because evaluating such efforts is difficult, especially for those external to the firm performing the research. R&D projects are a different sort of investment in that they generally do not take the form of a tangible asset that can be held as collateral. By contrast, investments in plant or equipment generally have physical assets that could be sold. But if an R&D project is unsuccessful, there may be little or nothing to show for one's investment. Companies that rely most heavily on outside financing such as small, technology-intensive startups would be particularly affected by this problem.

It is not clear, however, that capital markets have systematically avoided longer-term R&D (Teitelman 1993, 387). For example, advocates of technology policy often cite lower levels of venture capital funds around 1990 relative to earlier years as evidence that the federal government should fund more applied commercial R&D. But rather than being a permanent state of affairs, lower levels of venture capital may simply reflect a reaction to lower returns on earlier investments. If there are a limited number of "good" R&D projects or good project managers, we might expect to see a cycle of high returns to venture capital, followed by an influx of investment funds to a point where their volume is greater than the number of good projects, at which point returns would fall. Research suggests that such a cycle did occur (Florida 1994, 54).

Similar arguments have been used to justify federal support for high-risk R&D. Firms (or their investors) that are risk averse may find R&D projects less attractive than other types of investments, even if their potential returns are higher. And even for those firms that are not risk averse, knowing how long it will take to develop a new product or process, and thus how costly a project will be, is difficult. Those characteristics may be particularly evident for precompetitive R&D—those projects that have not developed sufficiently to make their commercial applications readily apparent. It is also hard to predict what magnitude of sales an innovation will attract, especially for those projects that could be useful across industries.

Encouraging Collaboration. Some authors have categorized the tendency to underinvest in certain risky or long-

11

term R&D as a market failure because if risks were pooled, the range of possible profits and losses associated with those R&D projects would be lower and there would be sufficient incentive to undertake more of them. The notion of pooling risks has led some analysts to argue that the federal government should encourage private firms and other organizations to form joint ventures for their research efforts. By eliminating duplication of effort, joint ventures can improve the returns on R&D investments for participants and perhaps encourage members to develop technical standards to share information with one another. In the case of Sematech, for example, collaborative efforts helped users of semiconductor manufacturing technology communicate their future plans and needs to suppliers of that equipment (CBO 1990, 15–39).

In the ATP's originating legislation, Congress indicated its interest in encouraging joint ventures with passages such as the following:

> Under the Program . . . the Secretary may . . .
> (1) aid industry-led United States joint research and development ventures . . . (which may also include universities and independent research organizations), including those involving collaborative technology demonstration projects which develop and test prototype equipment and processes. (U.S. Congress 1988, sec. 28[b][1])

It is not clear, however, that this policy was based solely on the economic rationales. It is also possible that joint ventures were encouraged to address a concern about the appearance of the program, that it "avoids providing undue advantage to specific companies" (U.S. Congress, 1988, sec. 28[a][2]).

In recent years, it appears that any number of firms have begun pursuing joint research projects of their own volition. But not every collaboration is appropriate, and it is not clear that joint projects established primarily for the sake of winning federal financial support will lead to more efficient R&D. Significant amounts of R&D take place among oligopolists and rivalrous market structures. With collaboration, R&D projects could be pulled out of their strategic context and undermine the advantage of certain companies by requiring them to share information with their competitors (Morone and Sassocio 1992, 61). Other participants may not trust the consortia with projects closest to their strategic interests, choosing projects of relatively low priority for collaboration (Werner and Bremmer 1991, 44). Nor is it clear whether collaboration has had its desired effect; some research suggests that subsidies that require cooperation seem to decrease rather than increase the amount of R&D conducted (Folster 1995, 403).[3]

Promoting U.S. Industry through Strategic Trade Policy. Under a line of argument known as strategic trade theory, the government could improve the nation's standard of living by directing federal resources toward particular key technologies. For certain manufacturing industries, economies of scale are so large that the world can accommodate only a few efficient producers (Krugman 1990). Federal R&D investments in those industries might allow U.S. businesses to develop innovations before foreign competitors and thereby earn above-average profits on their exports.

Some advocates of such a federal role also point to the R&D subsidies of other governments as the means by which foreign industries have been able to establish initial technological advantages that provided long-standing commercial benefits (Borrus 1993, 12). By establishing themselves as leaders in fields that exhibit large economies of scale and rapid innovation, foreign competitors have created first-mover advantages. In that sense, a policy of targeting federal support is a defensive strategy: if the United States fails to target certain technologies, it will be exceedingly difficult to catch up (CBO 1991, 5).

In 1991, Congress amended the legislation that created the ATP with the American Technology Preeminence Act. It included several passages about criteria for judging which firms would be eligible for ATP awards. Section 28 (d)(9) of the act, for example, states that:

> A company shall be eligible to receive financial assistance under this section only if:
>
> (A) the Secretary finds that the company's participation in the program would be in the economic interest of the United States, as evidenced by investments in the United States in research, development, and manufacturing . . . and
>
> (B) either
>
> (i) the company is a United States-owned company; or
>
> (ii) the Secretary finds that the company is incorporated in the United States and has a parent company which is incorporated in a country which affords to United States-owned companies opportunities, comparable to those afforded to any other company.

In part, those guidelines may have been intended to preclude embarrassing awards to foreign firms—especially those that might compete with U.S. companies. But in addition, the passage may reflect the notion that federal spending on commercial R&D projects might make the United States better off as in the context of the strategic trade theory. Critics of strategic trade policy contend that targeting is appropriate only in very few cases—the advantages of being the first to introduce an innovation are not always sustainable. Governments, it is argued, are notoriously poor at identifying the appropriate circumstances for targeting assistance, and while federal support might improve the competitive position of the recipient, it would be at the expense of other industries. Even under the most careful safeguards, it is often difficult to shield the process of making awards from political influences: "Finally, even economists who might be persuaded that high-technology industries make special contributions to national economic welfare are likely to remain highly skeptical about the ability of the American government to intervene effectively on their behalf" (Tyson 1992, 13). The implementation of the Advanced Technology Program provides a unique opportunity to determine whether this skepticism is warranted.

3
Can ATP Successfully Implement the Program?

The rationales discussed earlier suggest that there are justifiable economic reasons for the ATP: encouraging high-risk or long-term research, encouraging collaboration, and conducting a strategic trade policy. The debate over the rationales for government intervention in R&D and in markets more generally, however, involves two issues: the soundness of the rationales themselves and the ability of the government to implement programs to address those rationales. Strategic trade policy provides a good example. There appears to be agreement among many authors on the theoretical basis for strategic trade policy—that certain types of government interventions for certain industries might improve the fortunes of the nation. Many of those same authors, though, immediately introduce the caveat that government success in choosing the correct situations for the right industries is highly unlikely.

In this chapter, we look at the nuts and bolts of how the ATP has been carried out and analyze whether it has been implemented in a manner likely to address the economic rationales of the program. This approach allows us to go beyond the question of whether the program has reasonable goals and toward the question of what it takes to achieve those goals.

Background on the ATP

As of July 1996, the ATP had funded 280 projects in six general competitions and other competitions covering eleven focus areas. Nearly half the awards went to individual small businesses or to joint ventures led by small businesses (NIST 1996). About $970 million in federal money has been committed to ATP projects formed by private firms, some in collaboration with universities, not-for-profit organizations, and federal laboratories. The total amount of resources devoted to those projects, however, is at least twice that amount: award recipients are expected to provide at least 50 percent of project costs. Criticisms about inappropriate uses of government funds are less likely to be a problem when funding recipients also have a vested interest in the project's outcome. Similarly, ATP guidelines include restrictions on the amount of time over which a project can receive federal support, since it is hard to discontinue federal support for R&D projects.

Scientists and engineers—NIST employees and other experts from business, academia, research organizations, or other federal agencies such as the Advanced Research Projects Agency (ARPA), NASA, the Department of Energy, and the National Institutes of Health—evaluate each proposal for technical merit. Those projects that score well are reviewed by panels of business experts for the likelihood that the discovery can be "commercialized" successfully and its potential to result in broad economic benefits to the nation. This approach was designed to ensure that ATP awards are based on merit rather than on political influence.

ATP administrators make an explicit effort to evaluate their projects once awards are made. Recipients of federal funding are required to provide information several years following their award so that program managers can develop profiles of participants and the technologies involved, track progress, and try to assess whether industry has adopted R&D from ATP projects. It will take many years to accomplish this goal, however, since the primary focus of the evaluation deals with measuring the long-term economic effects of each project. According to program literature, ATP evaluators are looking for evidence of higher productivity among manufacturers that use new product or process technologies developed with federal assistance, as well as whether those developments offer higher quality or lower cost to their users.

Some of the features described above—cost sharing, an awards process based on technical merit, attempts at project evaluation—show that NIST has made significant efforts to avoid the problems of previous technology programs. But no matter how laudable, those efforts alone do not ensure the ATP's success.

To meet the ATP's goals, program managers need to succeed at two things: selecting projects with large returns to the nation and funding only those projects that would not otherwise find private financing. The first task involves looking for the biggest social returns on the federal dollar when making project awards. As for the second, there is no need to finance projects that the private sector would fund on its own.

Figure 3–1 shows how these two conditions might be illustrated. The horizontal dimension is a measure of how "good" the projects are, and in this case "good" is a measure of social benefits that include profits to the firm and those of any firms that imitate the technology (adjusted for the reduced profits of firms whose products are displaced), plus the value to consumers who benefit from lower prices or higher quality. "Good" projects have greater social benefits and are farther to the right along this dimension. The vertical dimension is a measure of expected private profitability, or the degree to which a firm (or investor) believes it can increase its economic return by initiating the R&D. Projects that are expected to be highly profitable would appear at the top of this scale.

In this figure, points in quadrant A represent hypothetical projects where the firm has sufficient incentive (expected profits) to fund the research and the R&D also generates social benefits. Since R&D often leads to bene-

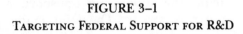

FIGURE 3-1
TARGETING FEDERAL SUPPORT FOR R&D

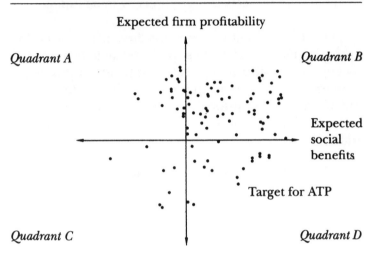

SOURCE: Authors.

fits beyond the firm that conducts the research, we expect most projects to fall in this quadrant. We can label these as good projects that would be done anyway. If the government funds projects that fall in this quadrant, it is simply displacing investment that the private sector would have pursued on its own.

Points in quadrant B represent those projects where the firm might make a profit but at a net cost to society. These could be termed bad projects that might be done anyway. An example might be efforts to improve techniques in counterfeiting currency. Those projects might lead to profits, but since governments, banks, and commercial entities have to invest in response to those efforts, society is worse off as a result.

Projects in quadrant C are not profitable for individual investors or firms or for the broader society. With the benefit of hindsight, we might place the Clinch River

Breeder Reactor, the supersonic transport, and some other projects in this category. The points in this quadrant represent bad projects that are unlikely to be funded privately.

Finally, quadrant D represents the target projects for a program like the ATP. These projects would benefit society but are not sufficiently profitable to attract private investment.[4] To the extent that the ATP is able to identify and provide funding to these projects, it is likely to address some of the rationales cited as the basis for this program.

Can ATP Pick the Right Projects?

Unfortunately, there is no reason to believe that firms will propose only projects with low profits and large social benefits to the ATP. In fact, we should expect firms to focus on the profitability of projects and to develop internal selection mechanisms to help differentiate among them on that dimension. Evaluating the expected level of profits from investments in R&D is challenging enough— there is little reason for firms to try to develop measures of the social benefits that might accrue to a project.

As a result, it is up to program administrators to develop and apply criteria that make it possible to solicit the appropriate projects from firms and then choose from among those projects the ones with the highest expected level of social benefits. This expectation means choosing "good" projects that the private sector would not undertake on its own.

The approach taken in this study is not based on an analysis of the economic or technological results of particular projects. There are significant problems with such analyses, including difficulties in identifying precisely what role the federal funding played in the final outcome and, in the case of ATP, its youth and thus the lack of mature projects. Instead, this volume closely examines how the ATP was implemented through three sets of documents: its originating legislation,[5] the regulations that helped form the program,[6] and its instructions to applicants.[7] Using these materials, we analyze whether the program is likely to be able to select projects with large social benefits that the private sector would not have undertaken on its own.

There are two parts to this analysis. The first is to ask whether the officials in charge of the program are able to develop and apply specific criteria that would allow them to home in on projects that are likely to fall in quadrant D of figure 3–1. The second is to examine whether the program's incentives concerning joint ventures, domestic economic growth, and intellectual property rights are consistent with the rationales of the program and promote focused areas of research.

Research That the Private Sector Would Not Undertake on Its Own. Although the authors of the legislation that created the ATP justified the program with some sound economic rationales, pursuing the goal of improving industry performance is no simple feat. In fact, Congress clearly recognized a potential problem with R&D programs like ATP—ensuring that it promotes additional research rather than simply subsidizing projects or joint ventures that would have found private funding on their own. The 1988 Omnibus Trade Act states that ATP administrators should:

> ensure that contracts . . . are not funding existing or planned research programs that would be conducted in the same time period in the absence of financial assistance under the Program. (U.S. Congress 1988, sec. 28[c][3])
> . . . the Program shall not make an award unless the award will facilitate the formation of a joint venture or the formation of a new research and development project by an existing joint venture. (U.S. Congress 1988, sec. 28[d][2])

21

It seems from these passages that Congress also recognized that funding additional projects was an important condition for the success of the program. To implement this aspect of the legislation, the regulations include language that calls for program administrators to consider the "degree to which ATP support is essential for the achievement of the broad based benefits. . . . This factor takes into consideration the likelihood of the results being achieved in the same general time frame by the applicant or by other U.S. researchers without ATP support" (NIST 1994b, 42).

In essence, the program is relying on firms to certify that federal funding adds to their investments or decreases the time that would be required to perform a research project. As the regulations suggest, it is not sufficient to ask whether the applicant would have performed the research during that time frame but whether other institutions would have pursued similar projects over the same period. These requirements are reiterated in the instructions to firms, with additional questions relating to how much the project would have to change without ATP funding (NIST 1994b, 19).

Imagine a firm's efforts to address those questions in its application. In some cases, the firm might have exhausted all other avenues of funding before applying to the ATP as a last resort. In other cases, the firm might have had too little internal funding to finance the project on its own but has made no attempt to secure outside funding. Finally, the firm might be quite interested in funding the project or could have received outside offers of funding the project but would prefer to use government assistance. The merits of government assistance are quite different in these three cases, but as long as the applicant states that the project would not proceed or would proceed at a slower pace without federal support, it passes the test. It is unreasonable to expect ATP administrators to try to determine which of these three cases applies to each project. The difficulties of that process suggest just how hard it is to create a mechanism that ensures federal funding will go to projects that the private sector would otherwise overlook.

Research That Leads to Large Social Benefits. The ATP legislation suggests that Congress intended for the program to address technologies that would be useful across industries, "for the purpose of assisting United States businesses in creating and applying generic technology and research results" (U.S. Congress 1988, sec. 28[a]).

Once Congress established the ATP, NIST administrators wrote regulations to guide the evaluation of the projects. Those criteria are grouped under the following broad headings and weighted in the selection process in the following manner:

- scientific and technical merit of the proposal, 30 percent
- potential broad-based economic benefits of the proposal, 20 percent
- adequacy of plans for eventual commercialization, 20 percent
- proposer's level of commitment and organizational structure, 20 percent
- experience and qualifications of the proposing organization, 10 percent (NIST 1994b)

The regulations, however, do not provide many specific clues about how to differentiate among projects. For example, the criteria in the category of "scientific and technical merit" are very general:

(i) Quality, innovativeness, and cost-effectiveness of the proposed technical program, i.e., uniqueness with respect to current industry practice. Applicants shall compare and contrast their approaches with those taken by other domestic

23

and foreign companies working in the same field.

(ii) Appropriateness of the technical risk and feasibility of the project; that is, is there a sufficient knowledge base to justify the level of technical risk involved, and is the risk commensurate with the potential payoff. Projects should press the state of the art while still demonstrating feasibility.

(iii) Coherency of technical plan . . .

(iv) Adequacy of systems integration . . .

(v) Potential broad impact on U.S. technology and knowledge base. (NIST 1994b, 42)

Moreover, there are few specific guidelines on ways to differentiate between projects that would be appropriate for firms and those that should be funded by the government. Firms have no reason to propose projects that best fit ATP goals rather than their own profitability. It would be surprising if a firm evaluated potential R&D projects on anything other than expected profit.

Within the ATP's regulations, the criteria that fall under the heading "potential broad-based economic benefits" are even more general:

(i) Potential to improve U.S. economic growth

(ii) Timeliness of proposal; that is, the potential project results will not occur too late or too early to be competitively useful.

(iii) Degree to which ATP support is essential for the achievement of the broad-based benefits from the proposed R&D and appropriateness of proposed R&D for ATP support . . .

(iv) Cost effectiveness of proposal. (NIST 1994b, 42)

While the regulations contain what appear to be reasonable criteria for evaluating projects, the rationale for government support for R&D suggests that only certain specific types of projects should be performed with public funds. There seems to be no indication in the regulations that the ATP has figured out a way to select those particular projects.

The ATP's instructions go beyond the regulations by specifying the types of projects that merit funding. For example, the questions regarding the "potential industries affected" and "the nature of the effect" begin to suggest the kinds of distinctions that would help differentiate between projects. In addition, the program's most recent instructions to applicants (NIST 1996, 6) ask firms to "link each technical capability which would result from the proposed R&D with the estimated, incremental economic benefits which would be realized."

The criteria, however, are not clear enough about two points that are key to promoting an effective federal role: is the private return low enough (so that the firm would not be interested on its own), and is the social return high enough (greater than other available public investments) (Averch 1993, 272)? Instead, the ATP's instructions emphasize the "macro" effects of specific technologies quite heavily: "Discuss the . . . implications of the technology for raising productivity, increasing economic growth, promoting high-quality employment, and improving quality of life" (NIST 1996, 6). Yet while R&D is important to economic growth, few individual technologies have a measurable impact on the growth rate, productivity, or standard of living in the U.S. economy as a whole. It is often quite difficult for firms to imagine the impact of their technology on their own industry; it is obviously much more difficult to imagine, much less quantify, the impact on other industries or on the economy as a whole.[8]

Unfortunately, the regulations or the instructions to firms do not provide firms with much guidance on how ATP projects might lead to broader benefits for society. It is only in the 1996 supplement to the *Proposal Preparation*

Kit that ATP includes a reference to the concept of spill-overs: "How cost sharing with ATP will . . . affect the potential for benefits accruing to others not participating directly in the project" (NIST 1996, 7).

The main problem is that the program has never established a clear distinction between the benefits to the firm that receives the funding and the broader benefits that society might gain from the investments. The benefits to society typically involve spillovers—the benefits to those firms or individuals that pay little or nothing for the research. In fact, it is because of these spillovers that there is a government role in funding certain efforts. One potential explanation for ATP's reluctance to address this issue is that it suggests the irony of a program that asks firms to propose projects whose benefits will accrue largely to others.

Emphasizing Particular Types of Projects. The instructions for applicants provide additional information on the particular types of projects of interest to ATP administrators. For example, the instructions give guidance on the types of risk of interest to ATP:

> ATP projects must press the state of the art and should involve significant technical challenges while still having credibility with respect to feasibility. A substantial number of proposals have been rejected by the ATP because they have insufficient technical risk. The ATP does not support projects for which the business risk is high but the technical risk is low. (NIST 1994b, 16)

But those instructions raise questions, such as the distinction between technical and business risks. Assuming that this distinction makes sense in practice, there are fundamental questions about the ATP emphasis on technical risk. For example, a firm may be close to completing work on an important technology (low technical risk) that has serious problems with intellectual property protection and, therefore, no easy path to commercialization (high business risk). This seems to be exactly the type of project that the government should be funding since there is a potentially high payoff to the nation but little incentive for the firm to invest. The ATP, however, suggests that it would score low against its criteria.

A second question involves how to score certain types of projects:

> Projects that do not involve technology development (e.g., those that emphasize development of voluntary consensus standards, data gathering/handbook preparation, or the testing of materials) tend not to score well against the ATP criteria. (NIST 1994b, 15)

It appears that this guidance may miss the point or, even worse, be contrary to the rationales behind federal funding of research. For example, some of the activities mentioned in the quotation may be the types of activities that should be supported by government funding— gathering and disseminating data, setting standards, and similar projects may have broad social benefits that private firms might find difficult to capture.[9] If those types of projects do not score well against the ATP criteria, then perhaps those criteria are not selecting the most appropriate projects.

Summary. The efforts of ATP administrators to target "good" projects provides an example of how easy it is to state the goals of the program, yet how difficult it can be to carry them out. One inherent obstacle is that the interests of the government and firms are very different. A firm would be better off if the government funded a project that it would have performed anyway. To expand social benefits truly, however, the government needs to choose those projects that firms would not undertake on their own. There is nothing wrong or particularly surprising that firms would prefer to have the government fund their R&D. The extent to which firms are able to predict even their own future profits from a project may be limited, and it seems unlikely to expect them to consider social benefits not directly relevant to their business. This reasoning is consistent with the findings of a recent evaluation of the program, where more than half of ATP applicants in the survey did not look elsewhere for funding before applying to ATP, and a smaller number of firms turned down offers of funding from private sources before applying to ATP (GAO 1996, 2).

Thus, to be successful, the ATP must be able to establish precise methods to measure the social returns of R&D projects. The language developed in the regulations and instructions, though, suggests that kind of precision is not possible. As a result, we would expect the program to fund projects that would have been performed without the ATP. This finding is also consistent with the GAO survey results, where half the respondents who did not receive ATP funding were able to continue the R&D project (GAO 1996, 4).[10]

4

Does ATP Create Incentives to Expand Social Benefits?

While the ATP has found it difficult to develop a method for choosing the right projects, the program might still achieve some of its goals by changing the incentives for participants so that they create more social benefits. Among the incentives that the ATP attempts to influence are encouraging joint ventures, promoting domestic economic growth, encouraging intellectual property protection, and promoting focused areas of research.

Encouraging Joint Ventures

From the program's inception, Congress sought to encourage joint ventures. ATP's originating legislation states that

> (b) Under the Program . . . the Secretary may . . .
> (1) aid industry-led United States joint research and development ventures . . . (which may also include universities and independent research organizations), including those involving collaborative technology demonstration projects which develop and test prototype equipment and processes. (U.S. Congress 1988, sec. 28[b][1])

According to ATP literature, the program has led to a number of joint ventures. Some of the language in the

29

legislation, however, suggests that including joint ventures in the ATP may have been more a defensive strategy than one designed to provide the right incentives: accordingly, joint ventures are emphasized in the ATP legislation, which states that the ATP should "avoid providing undue advantage to specific companies" (NIST 1992, 2–3).

Obviously, emphasizing joint ventures does not resolve the problem of providing an advantage to specific companies; it only provides a smaller advantage to a larger number of companies.

Creating incentives that encourage research organizations to form fruitful joint ventures has all the challenges, if not more, of selecting among proposals by individual companies. Because of the incentives that ATP provides for collaborators to pool their R&D efforts, some joint ventures could actually lead to a decrease in R&D investment. In some cases, that may lead to R&D that is performed more efficiently. In other situations, though, two competitors could be pulled away from their rivalrous context, perhaps resulting in less impetus to develop commercial applications for a technology as quickly as they would individually.

Other issues that must be addressed in funding joint ventures include the nationality and the status (firm, university, federal lab) and internal funding and indirect cost rates of the participants. As a result, hammering out agreements between ATP collaborators can require quite a lot of their time and attention—before the R&D even begins. The substantial increase in the volume of regulations and instructions that deal with joint ventures suggests just how difficult the process has been. For example, the 1996 changes to the instructions to firms state that:

> Based on feedback from companies involved in the ATP, we have found that organizing joint ventures is much more difficult than anticipated. Often the technical participants are able

to come to agreement quickly, but when attempts are made to get the concurrence of the companies' legal departments prior to the signing of the joint venture agreement, lengthy delays can occur, and sometimes joint ventures can unravel in spite of continuing enthusiasm on the part of the technical and business managers involved. (NIST 1996, 4)

These difficulties suggest that creating joint ventures in the United States is similar to some of the other goals of the program: it appears relatively easy to accomplish at first but much more difficult to accomplish in a meaningful way.[11]

Promoting Domestic Economic Growth

Another goal in the legislation that set up the ATP was to promote growth among U.S. firms relative to their foreign competitors. While much of the literature on strategic trade deals with the market structures and other conditions that might create the opportunity for government intervention to improve welfare, the ATP efforts appear to focus on preventing foreign firms from directly or indirectly benefiting from the program. For example, there is substantial material in the ATP statute and in the ATP regulations that deals with foreign business participation in federally sponsored projects (U.S. Congress 1988, sec. 28[d][9]; and NIST 1994b, 33–34). Much of that language states that award recipients must conduct their research in the United States and promote the domestic manufacture of any products resulting from the ATP funds, although foreign enterprises may participate in ATP projects as collaborative partners.

In addition to the practical difficulties involved in distinguishing between U.S. and foreign businesses, that goal can be at odds with some of the ATP's other objectives such as encouraging collaboration to improve the effi-

31

ciency of R&D. In some cases, the most appropriate partners might be those in another nation. Those preferential
arrangements might also be at odds with broader U.S. policy. For example, the regulations state that a company may
also be eligible if the country of the parent firm "affords
to United States-owned companies opportunities, compa-
rable to those afforded to any other company, to participate in any joint venture similar to those authorized under
the Program" (15 CFR Part 295.3).

A more fundamental problem, however, is that the
guidance applies best to those situations where the scope
of the R&D is narrow and the patents are most effective—in other words, when there is little need for public
funding. When those conditions are met, there are few
spillovers, and the private firms that receive the funding
can capture most of the benefits of their R&D. In those
situations where the R&D generates broad use across industries, efforts to restrict the benefits to domestic firms
are likely to be less successful.

Encouraging Intellectual Property Protection

One approach that the government might use to encourage more R&D is that used by the ATP: to help fund it,
thereby lowering the private sector's costs of undertaking
the project. Another approach is to help firms capture
more of the benefits from their research by granting them
tighter control over intellectual property rights. This too
is a tactic used in the ATP—those private sector firms selected for federal support are allowed to retain control
over intellectual property rights.

Interestingly, the extent of control over those rights
was expanded between the time that Congress created the
ATP and in later amendments to the original legislation.
The 1988 legislation stated:

> The federal government shall be entitled to
> a share of the licensing fees made to and re-

tained by any business or joint venture to which it contributes under this section in an amount proportional to the Federal share of the costs incurred by the business or joint venture as determined by independent audit. (U.S. Congress 1988, sec. 28[d][7])

In the 1991 amendments, this language was eliminated. According to the amendments, ATP participants are allowed to patent or copyright the results of an ATP project, but the federal government may reserve a nonexclusive license for the use of the technology (U.S. Congress 1988, sec. 28[d][11]). This change is consistent with the more general shift reflected in the Bayh-Dole Act, which encouraged small firms (and later all firms) to patent the results of government-sponsored research.[12]

Granting tighter control over intellectual property rights may encourage firms to conduct more R&D. But that goal may be at odds with another of the federal government: to disseminate the results of R&D so that its benefits flow to the economy as a whole. Firms and governments have quite different views on the best way to disseminate know-how.

Regardless of whether firms or the government funds the research, private organizations that develop the technology are likely to try to capture the maximum benefits for themselves. In situations where market rivalry and spillovers lead to widespread adoption of a technology (albeit keeping the developing firm from fully appropriating its returns), there may be benefits for the nation. In other situations, though, the social benefits might be significantly larger if the technology were distributed more widely. In these cases, the government might prefer a different course from that practiced by the firm, and we would expect a successful program to have the ability to influence the outcome in these cases. The regulations drawn up to administer ATP, though, send mixed messages: although they suggest that firms promote widespread use of the technologies developed with ATP financing, the program also encourages award recipients to protect the intellectual property. Projects are to be judged by the

> degree to which the proposal identifies potential applications of the technology and provides evidence that the applicant has credible plans to assure prompt and widespread use of the technology if the R&D is successful and to ensure adequate protection of the intellectual property by the participant(s), and as appropriate, by other U.S. businesses. (NIST 1994b, 43)

The instructions also provide information on the way that ATP expects the technology to be developed:

> ATP award recipients are encouraged to protect ownership of the technology developed in the ATP project so that the work will benefit the U.S. economy. You are not required to share the technology with the public or with other companies, unless you choose to do so. Explain how you will protect the intellectual property rights and trade secrets so that the incentive to commercialize is preserved and the benefits of the ATP-sponsored work accrue to the U.S. (NIST 1994b, 20)

Presumably those arrangements were established to broaden the incentives for private firms to participate in the program and put their own money on the line. A broader question, however, is whether there is common ground between the government's interests in disseminating technology and the firms' interests in maximizing profits through control over the dissemination of the technology. This kind of problem would not be so difficult to manage in the case of government support of universities, since universities also have an interest in and a mechanism for disseminating technical results.

Governments have a role in ensuring that intellectual property rights are sufficient to encourage firms to risk their funds. In those situations where this type of protection cannot be achieved, the government may choose to invest its own funds to create the technology. Once the government invests its funds through a program like the ATP, however, encouraging firms to protect their intellectual property may run counter to the program's goal of promoting broad social benefits. By allowing firms to hold exclusive rights to inventions that have been generated at public expense, it seems to require the public to pay twice for the same invention.[13]

Promoting Focused Areas of Research

In 1994, the ATP signaled a change in the nature of the competitions from general competitions to focused programs:

> While the ATP will continue to hold general competitions, a major change being implemented in 1994 is the initiation of focused programs. . . . Programs generally involve the parallel development of a suite of interlocking projects. By using programs to manage groups of projects that complement and reinforce each other, the ATP can have the greatest possible impact on technology and the economy. (NIST 1994b, 3)

The first focus area awards were made in October 1994. The focus areas and the dollar amounts of the awards are shown in table 4–1. Additional focus area awards were made in November 1994 (one), July 1995 (one), August 1995 (three), and September 1995 (six). In some of these cases, however, additional awards were made to projects in existing focus areas.

Focus areas for federal support may provide evidence of a concerted effort toward pursuing a strategic trade pol-

TABLE 4-1
ATP FOCUS AREAS, 1994–1995
(millions of current dollars)

Title	Description	Date	Number of Awards	ATP Funds ($)
Component-based software	Develop reusable components for the custom software market	10/94 9/95	11 7	40.4 13.9
Information infrastructure for health care	Build libraries of patient records, clinical diagnostic support	10/94 9/95	16 10	51.6 62.9
Tools for DNA diagnostics	Speed up sequence interpretation methods	10/94 7/95	13 7	56.4 22.6
Technologies for the integration of manufacturing applications	Affordable manufacturing software systems	7/95 10/94	7 1	22.6 1.9
Manufacturing composite structures	Automate processing for designing weaves of composite fibers	11/94 9/95	6 7	17.6 14.7

Vapor compression refrigeration technology	Improve fuel efficiency of air conditioning; refrigeration systems; aid CFC phaseout	8/95	7	12.7
Digital data storage	Encourage collaboration in compression/storage R&D	8/95	6	38.1
Materials processing for heavy manufacturing	Demonstrate manufacturing processes that prohibit corrosion	8/95	8	19.9
Catalysis and biocatalysis technologies	Develop new catalysts for chemical manufacturing processes	9/95	9	50.7
Motor vehicle manufacturing technology	Decrease span from new car design to manufacturing	9/95	15	54.2
Digital video in information networks	Help set standards, improve interoperability among digital video technology developers	9/95	6	55.0

NOTE: A new focus area for 1997 is called issue engineering.
SOURCE: NIST.

icy. But it is not clear that program administrators selected the eleven technology fields by using the characteristics described in the literature about strategic trade—that is, manufacturing industries with very large economies of scale in production. ATP literature states only that administrators identified focus areas based on industry input; there is little indication why program managers believe those technologies are important. Nor is there much information in ATP's booklets about how one applies to win some of the funds set aside for the focus areas. Program instructions merely state that competitions within focus areas are run in the same manner as the general competitions, except that the proposals are limited to the eleven technical areas (NIST 1994b, 1).

Focus areas offer some potential advantages for the program administrators. For example, such a strategy would reduce the range of expertise needed to evaluate proposals. In the general competitions, ATP managers would require the help of a large number of experts to evaluate proposals. But before making awards, administrators also need to make choices among projects that are each rated highly in their field of technology. Given the types of criteria ATP has outlined, these choices are not likely to be easy. In addition, it may be difficult to call on such wide-ranging specialists regularly to perform those types of project evaluations. ATP provided a hint at this when it stated that the time required to make selections in focus area competitions is expected to be considerably shorter than in general competitions (NIST 1994a, 10). In addition, the volume of funds available had increased sharply since the first years, which led to an increase in both the average award and the number of awards in 1994 and 1995 over the previous years.

The shift to focus areas also leads to some difficulties for the program administrators. The most obvious is how to choose the focus areas. Industry input sounds reasonable, but as noted above, firms are expected to be most interested in those developments that will provide them an advantage in their markets and increase their profits. These are not the same projects of the greatest interest to the government. And the particular technologies identified for support are likely to depend on which industry ATP talks to the most. There may be no systematic way to solicit objective comments from industry rather than focusing on their areas of vested interest. In short, picking focus areas appears to be at least as problematic as picking projects.

There is also a potential danger in ATP's shift to focus areas. As we argue in this volume, ATP has devised a procedure that may not guarantee the selection of the projects with the greatest social benefits. Nevertheless, thus far the program's process for selecting awards appears to be insulated from political pressures. The move to focus areas may jeopardize this outcome because the selection process has become less transparent than it is for general competitions. Moreover, the dollar amounts set aside for focus areas are much larger—some targeted technologies receive as much as $50 million annually, while the average size of projects awarded in general competitions has been in the neighborhood of $2 million. Combined with the fact that many industries are geographically concentrated, ATP's move to emphasizing focus areas may make the program more vulnerable to political pressures.

5
Conclusions

The origins of the Commerce Department's Advanced Technology Program grew out of slowing productivity growth over the past two decades and political dissatisfaction with the economic performance of U.S. industries relative to foreign competition. Traditionally, federal programs directed support for R&D toward particular missions such as promoting basic research, toward products that ultimately the government planned to procure, or toward research that helped set standards for industries or disseminate know-how. The ATP, however, was designed explicitly to promote economic growth in civil industries and was closely tied to the rationales for government intervention in R&D activity for the purpose of improving industrial performance.

Some of the stronger economic rationales for the ATP are closely related to the traditional arguments for federal support of R&D. Private businesses may not invest enough in precompetitive or generic technologies because broad spillovers preclude the firm from appropriating its full returns or the costs of investment are beyond the means of a single company. By leveraging private resources for R&D and encouraging firms and other organizations to collaborate, the ATP might expand the amount of R&D conducted on high-risk, generic technologies. Other economic rationales also appear to have influenced the design of the ATP. For example, some of the ATP's original goals appear to be grounded in strategic trade theory—in particular, the notion that by targeting federal funding toward certain key technologies, U.S. businesses might be able to develop innovations before their foreign competitors and earn above-average returns on that R&D through exports.

Many of the authors responsible for those theoretical arguments about government intervention, however, argue that such targeting is appropriate only in a few circumstances and that the federal government is unlikely to identify those situations well. Similarly, the federal government may not be able to keep foreign firms from benefiting from the projects it helps to finance given the volume of foreign direct investment and level of international collaboration among firms.

Those critiques suggest that even with some sound economic rationales, the effectiveness of the ATP depends on whether the program can be successfully implemented. By looking at the nuts and bolts of the program—the regulations and the instructions to firms—we analyzed whether the program was able to target funding toward projects with broad social benefits or create incentives for that type of R&D.

Based on our review, the program seems to have had only limited success. As guidelines for the program show, the ATP emphasizes factors such as expected future sales and job creation when selecting projects, rather than looking for situations where there is likely to be a large gap between social and private rates of return. While allowing recipients of federal funding to keep intellectual property rights on the results of ATP projects may increase the pool of applicants, that policy may also constrict the social benefits associated with that R&D. And by emphasizing commercial potential when choosing among applicants, the ATP is likely to be selecting projects that could also obtain financing through the private sector.

Two possibilities explain those difficulties in implementing the program. First, the goals of government and firms conflict. The federal government's interest lies in funding technologies that would not be of sufficient interest to the private sector, but firms would have little interest in or ability to propose projects that differ significantly from the projects they pursue for profit. The only way to ensure that this difference will not create problems is to develop some way to predict profits and social benefits and pick only those projects where government support will be beneficial. Unfortunately, this effort is complicated by the fact that predicting the likely profits of R&D efforts is enormously difficult and is arguably much easier than predicting the social benefits.[14]

Second, there is no common ground between many of the political and the economic requirements of a successful program. For example, one way to resolve some of the economic problems is to identify areas where appropriability problems are most severe, as in industries where intellectual property protection is known to be ineffective. That kind of targeting, however, would reduce the possible constituency of the programs since industries without those kinds of appropriability problems would have little reason to support the program politically. Similarly, the economic importance to the government of disseminating results widely and without cost runs into the political opposition of the firms and also risks providing benefits to foreign firms—a potentially embarrassing outcome politically.

The ATP provides an interesting experiment in whether the government can promote economic growth through an explicit technology policy. Only projects with certain characteristics will enable ATP to achieve its economic goals, and those may not be the same projects that help it achieve political support. Given the difficulties we identified in carrying out such a technology policy and Congress's recent efforts to eliminate the program, it appears that the overlap between programs that expand social benefits and those that are politically successful is very small indeed.

Notes

1. Many of the researchers that have consistently found a high social return to private R&D expenditures, however, have not found similarly high rates for public R&D spending (Nadiri 1993, 10; OTA 1986, 14).

2. Some federal investments in technology for commercial purposes did occur before this period. Many of these investments are described by Cohen and Noll (1991).

3. Folster's empirical results are ambiguous. On the one hand, they might simply indicate that collaborators conduct R&D more efficiently. On the other hand, the lower level of R&D might also indicate moral hazard problems, reduced competition, or other disincentives.

4. Collaboration might also make some of these projects profitable in that an entity consisting of a number of firms likely to benefit from a technology might profitably support the R&D, while individual firms may have insufficient knowledge of other applications or an inability to capture the gains due to lack of intellectual property protection.

5. Omnibus Trade and Competitiveness Act of 1988 (Pub. L. 100–418, 15 U.S.C. 278n) as amended by the American Technology Preeminence Act of 1991 (Pub. L. 102–245).

6. ATP Rule, 15 CFR Part 295.

7. The November 1994 "Advanced Technology Program Proposal Preparation Kit" was the primary source for this analysis, although some of the relevant changes published in the May 1996 update have been noted. We also consulted previous versions of the proposal preparation kits that were published in February 1994 and in 1992.

8. Nathan Rosenberg discusses the difficulty of anticipating the uses of a new technology in both general terms and in the context of a particular industry (1994).

9. In fact, the legislation mentions some of these types of efforts in the context of the discussion of joint ventures that would qualify for funding (U.S. Congress 1991, sec. 28[b]).

10. It is possible that some of the applicants who nearly won ATP funding benefited from a "halo effect" that made it easier to attract attention and funding from private sources. One might interpret this,

however, as further evidence that the ATP is attracting projects that the private sector expects will be profitable in the future, rather than those that are of interest because of their large social benefits.

11. Survey-based results also show that few joint ventures (33 percent) continue with projects if they are not successful in winning ATP funding, while 58 percent of single applicants continue with the projects (GAO 1996, 6).

12. Eisenberg (1996), p. 3.

13. Ibid.

14. Krugman (1991) has suggested that economists should abandon any attempt to measure knowledge spillovers, as they leave no paper trail (p. 53). The requirement here is even more difficult since it involves *predicting* knowledge spillovers.

Bibliography

American Association for the Advancement of Science. 1996. *Congressional Action on Research and Development in the FY 1997 Budget, R&D Budget and Policy Project.* Washington, D.C.: AAAS.

Averch, Harvey A. 1993. "Criteria for Evaluating Research Projects and Portfolios." In *Evaluating R&D Impacts: Methods and Practice,* edited by Barry Bozeman. Norwell, Mass.: Kluwer Academic Publishers.

BEA. 1994. "A Satellite Account for Research and Development." *Survey of Current Business* (November): 37–71.

Borrus, Michael. 1993. "Industrial Policy American Style." *International Economic Insights* 4 (2), (March–April).

Branscomb, Lewis. 1992. "Does America Need a Technology Policy?" *Harvard Business Review* 70: 24–31.

CBO. 1990. *Using R&D Consortia for Commercial Innovation: SEMATECH, X-Ray Lithography, and High-Resolution Systems.* Washington, D.C.: U.S. Congressional Budget Office.

———. 1991. *Targeting Emerging-Technology Industries.* Washington, D.C.: U.S. Congressional Budget Office.

Cohen, Linda, and Roger Noll. 1991. *The Technology Pork Barrel.* Washington, D.C.: Brookings Institution.

Council on Competitiveness. 1991. *Gaining New Ground: Technology Priorities for America's Future.* Washington, D.C.: Council on Competitiveness.

Eisenberg, Rebecca. 1996. "Public Research and Private Development: Patents and Technology Transfer in the Human Genome Project." *University of Virginia Law Review* 82: 1663.

Florida, Richard. 1994. "Keep Government Out of Venture Capital." In *Financing Entrepreneurs,* edited by Cynthia Beltz. Washington, D.C.: AEI Press.

Folster, Stefan. 1995. "Do Subsidies to Cooperative R&D Actually Stimulate R&D Investment and Cooperation?" *Research Policy* 24: 403–17.

GAO. 1996. January *Performance Measurement: The Advanced Technology Program and Private Sector Funding,* GAO-RCED-96-47. Washington, D.C.: U.S. General Accounting Office.

Krugman, Paul. 1983. "Targeted Industrial Policies: Theory and Evidence." In *Industrial Change and Public Policy.* Federal Reserve Bank of Kansas City: 123–55.

———. 1990. *Rethinking International Trade.* Cambridge, Mass.: MIT Press.

———. 1991. *Geography and Trade.* Cambridge, Mass.: MIT Press.

Morone, Joseph, and Damian Sassocio. 1992. "A Success-based Competitiveness Policy." *Issues in Science and Technology* 9 (2), (Winter 1992–1993): 61–72.

Mowery, David, and Nathan Rosenberg. 1989. *Technology and the Pursuit of Economic Growth.* New York: Cambridge University Press.

Nadiri, Ishaq. 1993. "Innovations and Technological Spillovers." Cambridge, Mass.: National Bureau of Economic Research working paper 4423.

National Science and Technology Council. 1995. *National Security Science and Technology Strategy.* Washington, D.C.: National Science and Technology Council.

Neu, C. R., and Michael Kennedy. 1993. *Do We Need Special Federal Programs to Aid Defense Conversion?* Santa Monica, Calif.: RAND.

NIST. 1992. *ATP Proposal Preparation Kit: Proposal Solicitations ATP 92-01 and 93-01.* Gaithersburg, Md.: National Institute of Standards and Technology.

———. 1994a. *ATP Proposal Preparation Kit.* Gaithersburg, Md.: National Institute of Standards and Technology.

————. 1994b. *ATP Proposal Preparation Kit.* Gaithersburg, Md.: National Institute of Standards and Technology.

————. 1995. "Announcements, ATP Publications." ATP Homepage (http://www.atp.nist.gov/). Gaithersburg, Md.: National Institute of Standards and Technology.

————. 1996. *ATP Proposal Preparation Kit Supplement.* Gaithersburg, Md.: National Institute of Standards and Technology.

OTA. 1986. *Research Funding as an Investment.* Washington, D.C.: U.S. Office of Technology Assessment.

Rosenberg, Nathan. 1994. *Exploring the Black Box: Technology, Economics and History.* New York: Cambridge University Press.

Schacht, Wendy. 1995. *R&D Partnerships: Government-Industry Collaboration.* Washington, D.C.: Congressional Research Service 95-499-SPR.

Silber and Associates. 1996. *Survey of Advanced Technology Program 1990–1992 Awardees: Company Opinion about the ATP and Its Early Effects.* Clarksville, Md.: Silber and Associates.

Teitelman, Robert. 1993. "Wall Street and the New Economic Correctness." *Institutional Investor,* February: 36–44.

Tyson, Laura D'Andrea. 1992. *Who's Bashing Whom? Trade Conflict in High Technology Industries.* Washington, D.C.: Institute for International Economics.

U.S. Congress. 1988. *Omnibus Trade and Competitiveness Act* (Pub. L. 100418, August 23, Title VI, "Advanced Technology").

————. 1992. *American Technology Preeminence Act of 1991* (Pub. L.102-245, February 14, Title II, "Advanced Technology Program").

Weidenbaum, Murray. 1992. "Sponsoring Research and Development." *Society* 29 (July–August): 39–47.

Werner, Jerry, and Jack Bremer. 1991. "Hard Lessons in Cooperative Research." *Issues in Science and Technology* 7 (3) (Spring): 44–49.

White House. 1993. *Technology for America's Economic Growth.* Washington, D.C.: White House.

About the Authors

LOREN YAGER is assistant director with the Office of the Chief Economist, U.S. General Accounting Office. He is responsible for providing economic advice and assistance to GAO divisions on topics such as technology and trade issues. Before joining GAO in 1992, Mr. Yager was an economic analyst at RAND, where he was the author of studies on high-technology trade and U.S.-Japan trade policy issues. He has also held positions as an economist with the Aerospace Research Center and the Bureau of Labor Statistics in Washington, D.C. He is a graduate of Johns Hopkins University and holds an M.A. from the University of Maryland and a Ph.D. from the RAND Graduate School.

RACHEL SCHMIDT is a principal analyst in the National Security Division of the Congressional Budget Office, where she researches issues in weapons procurement, research and development, strategic mobility, the defense industrial base, and acquisitions policy. Before joining CBO, she was an economist with the Economics and Statistics Administration of the U.S. Department of Commerce and an economic analyst with RAND. At RAND, she was the author or co-author of studies on defense profit policy and its relationship with capital investment, maintaining combat aircraft design capability in an era of lower defense spending, and U.S. export control policy. She is a graduate of Virginia Polytechnic Institute and State University and holds an M.A. from the University of Chicago and a Ph.D. from the RAND Graduate School.